MW00413421

THE COUNTRY OF WOMEN

THE
COUNTRY
OF
WOMEN

POETRY BY SANDRA KOHLER

CALYX BOOKS • CORVALLIS, OREGON

The publication of this book was supported by a grant from the Lannan Foundation.

© Copyright 1995 Sandra Kohler

No part of this book may be reproduced in whole or in part without written permission of the publisher except in reviews or critical writing.

Cover art by Shelly Corbett
Cover and book design by Cheryl McLean

CALYX Books are distributed to the trade through **Consortium Book Sales and Distribution, Inc., St. Paul, MN.**

CALYX Books are also available through major library distributors, jobbers, and most small press distributors including: Airlift, Banyan Tree, Bookpeople, Inland, Pacific Pipeline, and Small Press Distribution. For personal orders or other information contact: CALYX Books, PO Box B, Corvallis, OR 97339, (503) 753-9384, FAX (503) 753-0515.

∞

The paper in this book meets the guidelines for permanence and durability of the Committee on Production Guidelines for Book Longevity of the Council on Library Resources and the minimum requirements of the American National Standard for the Permanence of Paper for Printed Library Materials z32.48-1984.

Library of Congress Cataloging-in-Publication Data

Kohler, Sandra, 1940-
    The country of women / by Sandra Kohler.
        p. cm.
    ISBN 0-934971-46-3 : $21.95. — ISBN 0-934971-45-5 (pbk.) : $11.95
    1. Women—Poetry.   I. Title.
    PS3561.03577C68   1995
    811'.54—dc20   95-5304
                                                              CIP

CKNOWLEDGMENTS

Acknowledgment is made to the following publications in which these poems were previously published: "Trying to Talk About Sex–II" and "Last Poem from Squaw Valley" in *The American Poetry Review*, July–August 1988; "Trying to Talk About Sex–I" in *The Massachusetts Review*, Vol. XXXI, No. 3, Autumn 1990; "Mountains" in *The American Poetry Review*, September–October 1991; "Craving" and "Bread" in *West Branch*, No. 30, 1992; one section of "Ars Poetica Feminae" in *CALYX Journal*, Winter 1992/1993, Vol. 14, No. 2, as "Vessel"; "Stew" in *5 AM*, No. 6, 1993; "How We Grow" in *West Branch*, Issue No. 31/32, February 1993; "Sixth Day" in *Sojourner*, June 1993; "Distantiation" (there titled "Detached"), "Desire," and "In the Dark" in *Northeast Corridor,* Fall–Winter 1993; "The Country of Women," "California Desert Song," and "The Dream" in *Calapooya Collage*, No. 18, August 1994; and "Equestrian" in *Flyway,* Issue No. 1, May 1995.

For Walter

*and in memory of my parents,
Frances Isenberg Iger
and Philip A. Iger*

*T*ABLE OF CONTENTS

ROLOGUE

ARS POETICA FEMINAE

Ars Poetica Feminae

I.

Even the oaks with their crimson bunches
of leaves are blue this morning in the glaze
of cold rain. One bone in my body,
throbbing stick, echoes the rain.
There are clouds where my breasts should be,
heavier than leaves, layers of darkness piled
on beds where impatiens still bloom,
pale stars, small angry flowers. I'm closed down:
shut bud, low sky, the eye of a hibernating
animal; living in empty weather, an exile
from the country that fed me, stony breast
that gave me suck. Will the spring's
resinous waters spill over me again, pungent foam,
salt, bubbling, brimming to the lips?
Closing my eyes, drifting, I hear a cat stalking,
black, fierce, lovely. My daemon
cast out but hunting me.

II.

The poem comes to the man who is ready for her,
that famous poet said, the man who waits,
vessel, temple, emptied, open as dawn.
But how does a poem come to a woman? The woman
who waits for a poem is scrubbing a floor, packing
lunches, vacuuming the study of a man who waits

for a poem. She is waiting for a poem, wrapped
in an old bathrobe, listening to her child cough
in his sleep, waiting to see if he's well enough
for school, or if her day of waiting will be spent
playing Parchesi, wiping up spills, reading
about samurai. In the bluish dawn, gazing
into the silver kalanchoe hanging at the window,
she notices a cluster of drooping leaves—
does it need water, food, is the light too strong
for it? The woman who waits for a poem lives
in a world calling her every instant: keep me alive.
Let her wake empty as a shell, blank as a coin
rubbed over and over by the days, each dawn
that world fills her, each dawn etches her.

III.

Why wouldn't a woman be good
at waiting for the poem?
She's trained to wait
from cradle to grave.
Waiting to be old enough,
waiting to be a woman,
waiting to be asked,
waiting for the telephone call,
waiting for the blood
every month,
waiting nine months
for a child,
waiting for a man
to come home from work,
waiting for a child

to come home from school,
waiting for the babies
to fall asleep,
waiting for the angry man
to walk off his rage,
waiting for the happy man
to surface from the work
of his happiness—
why shouldn't a woman
so schooled in waiting
wait for the poem
so skillfully
that the poem feels itself
forced out
into the world
where a woman waits for it?

IV.

The poem comes to the man who is ready for her.
How does a woman summon herself? For centuries,
this woman waiting for a poem has been called
poem. Casting off her old bathrobe,
her responsibilities, would her body give off
light, become crescent moon, muse?

A woman is not a poem. The poem is not a woman.
The poem is what we discover in the waiting,
what we dredge or dream or babble like sleepers
out of the dark. The poem is what we meet
like a lover, what dogs us like a nagging spouse,
a whining child. The poem is a cruelty

we inflict which is also inflicted upon us.
The poem is what we make of the raw food,
the recalcitrant body of our lives.

V.

The air this morning, soft, damp,
sustaining. The black streets wet with a sheen
not quite dew. The street lights, small signals
burning when everything sleeps,
live embers, watch-fires. The lawn
lying open to the darkness
and the darkness masking it the way
a lover lies down on the white body
of his beloved. The blood receding
from my face, the blood gathering
at the center of my body to pour out
slowly. My nipples alive and speaking
milk, my warm thighs, closed as if
each white curve were marble. My child
stirring and softly groaning, the silent
birds, the dawn pale and blank as a woman
waking to loss, something missing.
The breathless litany of the leaves
betraying what stalks them.

 PART ONE

MOUNTAINS

# MOUNTAINS

*For my sister,
Roseann Waldstein*

1. THE JOURNEY:
TO A FRIEND CLIMBING KILIMANJARO

This is the first day of your journey
to the mountains, to the final
mountain, Kilimanjaro.
Last summer in the Sierra Nevada
I learned the names of peaks:
Beatitude, Heavenly, Northern Fruit.
For the first time I understood
the need to scale rock, reach a place
where vision is all that matters.
Every day we murmur to ourselves
"this is all that matters"—
"my child is well," "I'm healthy,"
"my husband loves me"—
but living in the valleys
you and I know everything counts,
we could be ruined,
sacked like old cities, destroyed
by disasters we can't even augur.
There is a time for leaving the valley
where our lives, dense as gardens,
proliferate for years, tangles
of blossoming chaos.
There is a time for climbing mountains,

as you are climbing Kilimanjaro,
ascending the slopes whose names
I invent: Solitude, Dangerous Joy,
Pathways of the Last Ascent.
There is a time for learning
the lung's hunger as the air thins
and the body, condensing,
becomes mineral, splendid,
a jewel astonished by something
within us, a streak of light.

II. WAKING IN THE VALLEY

A scent of disorder wakes me,
unpredicted weather.
Because either the rain
stopped falling or stopped
falling audibly or I stopped
being able to hear the fall
of rain, I am left with only
my body to listen to.
Lying in the dark I am aware
there is blood in my veins,
that my body fills a space
that could be empty.
I wonder what is written
on the face I have never seen.
I stretch out on the skin
of darkness, touch it,
lover, explorer.
It is thick, sustaining
as the fell of an animal
a whole culture lives on.

We eat this illusion
every day, we cover
our unfinished bodies
with its harsh fur, we make
weapons and icons
of its fine bones.
It fails to give us
a mirror, a light, a way out.

III. SEASONS

Thirty years ago it was the indigo
of twilight that was my country,
now the intensities of dawn.
The blue behind the evergreens
is harsher than the rich relinquishments
of spring evenings.
How can I love this unpropitious hour?
Twilight leads us to presences
which break the young heart
to be remade by decades
of morning's bitter draught, heal-all.
Choosing, I would choose to die
in the morning, after first light,
in the cold clarity
of a month like March.
I would also choose not to die.
The oldest woman I know
does not feel old enough to want
to die. Spring still calls her
to the frozen furrows of her garden
to sow early sweet peas, her legs
gnarled roots, her eyes startlingly new.

IV. THREE WOMEN
AND A MOUNTAIN

The slow games of the body are playing
without me this morning: I am here
and not here. My womb is empty
and I am emptier, an absence floating
above a space, a vacant room
swollen with the unshed web
of unconceived possibility.
I think of my sister, a woman
discovering late in middle age
how to climb mountains,
of my friend on the other side
of the earth, sleeping this morning
on the slopes of Kilimanjaro.
We are women whose bodies
have reached a verge:
no longer breeding grounds, nurseries.
Each of us has been on the mountain
for years, stalled at the base camp,
beginning to ascend sidewise,
crabbed, almost imperceptibly
inching up till we suddenly realize
these are the high slopes:
Solitude, Dangerous Joy,
Pathways of the Last Ascent.
Each of us finds herself
on a ledge, stony outcropping,
precipitous, a place
we must transform from extremity
to a part of the journey.

V. A RETURN

A woman comes back at dawn
to the house she lives in.
She is wearing the lucid gown of evening
washed with the iridescent stream
of the city's lights;
her face wears itself like a corsage;
she is bearing the scent
crushed out of the night gardens
by April, then May;
the shock of jasmine comes into
the hall with her skirts
on the breath of first light
dense as pollen, as the dust
grainy centuries have given back
again and again.
Coming home at dawn
bearing the night
she is warrior,
she is voyager, the darkness
scatters at her feet.
She is the one who went farther
than had been known,
who returned and lived.

PART TWO

SIX FROM SQUAW VALLEY

FLYING WEST

When I left home a child
told me to come back and bring him
the truth about the West.
This morning over the badlands
I discover spies, cowboys, lovers
hiding out in the hills
through that blind mirror
where I see myself desirable,
nubile as a continent.

The badlands are another mirror,
lying beneath me, furled,
enfolded, the lips of a sex.
Spies, cowboys, lovers lie.
The truth is I know a man
who knows how to love me
the way he loves the badlands,
caresses them with his camera
the way he tongues my sex.
He is the man who can love
a country he doesn't own.

In the Dark

From the balcony the half-moon's
half hidden by a drift of cloud.
There's a woman in this house
so like my friend B.
that trying to remember B.'s face
tonight I see only hers.
Is this the failure of memory—
always overlaid by a present
that wakes and obscures it at once?
The stars are surfacing
the way the bed of a river
comes clear after long gazing
into deep water.
Which of that stand of pines
between me and the mountains
and the moon is nearest?
Each of them rising
blots out a forest
on that mountain on the horizon.

All I remember of the dead
are moments of memory.
Now the moon's dark half
perfects it with its darkness.
Beneath a dog's mechanical barking,
beneath the occasional plane scoring
a line of sky
the shiver of moving water
precipitates out of silence.
I'm filling with tears.
Before this longing
what was there?

$\mathcal{T}$RYING TO TALK ABOUT SEX – I

For days I've been thinking about sex.
Not the exuberant sexual
flowering of this valley,
the bluest forget-me-not's intricate lips,
the poppy's bravado,
the Jeffrey pine's candy-store perfume
that opens like childhood when you hug it—
not this. And not sex as great metaphor, the force
that formed even the granite ridge
I scrambled down, scared numb, this afternoon,
fields of stony waves, fruition, another sea.
And not the primal sexual world
of the animals, even the ones we dream,
the rattlesnake my fear saw under every boulder
and met in the small hours,
shrunk and misshapen, on an iron stair.
Not even the sexual halo, beauty,
the light on and of our bodies
clearest in children, breathing pearls.
All day they've been my small tormentors,
teasing out my longing for my faraway son.
Riding the chair lift over chasms,

the only landscape I saw
was the one shattered in him
if the cables snapped.
How do I dare live dangerously?
I want to tell the truth: sex is not
the final intimacy for me.
It's easier to take off my clothes than read a poem;
I'd sooner have sex with a man
than loosen my bowels in front of him;
I'd rather open my thighs to a stranger
than leave him alone with my son for an hour.
I don't understand why sex is so frightening
that we must own each other.
Coming down the mountain
every step I took seemed a risk.
Finally fear wore through, numbed, used up:
I fell into rhythm, moved with the stones.
I wanted to simply talk about sex,
about the meeting bodies of women and men
as if those bodies were objects, outside nature.
Everything I say bears witness against me.

CHARLIE, ALMOST EIGHT

When I left you told me to bring you back
the truth about the Old West.
Spy, small inquisitor,
you need to know everything:
who phoned, what's that letter, why'd you just sigh.
Now, a continent away, reading breakfast,
you stall over comics and honey,
a dreaming bee.

Last week you made
a birdwatcher's journal,
dragged a kitchen chair out to the sidewalk
in front of our scrap of lawn
and recorded your first sighting:
one pigeon.

Everything nourishes you.
I want to celebrate your pitching arm,
Pinto All-Star, your persistence:
how at four you'd take nineteen shots
at a basket five times your height
and sink the twentieth.

How can I tell what you weigh,
feeding root, anchor, ball and chain?
There are days you run me into the sky;

a soaring kite, I levitate.
At two and a half your tantrum one morning
drained me to solid rage:
I was Jahweh, I saw you ruined,
wanted to rip you up like a canvas, begin again.

The night you sobbed till you vomited,
"Why do I have to die?"
I held you in comfortless arms
till you fell asleep the way I'll die,
exhausted, unreconciled.
After that you never let me sing
the cherry song at bedtime—you couldn't hear
"the story that I love you, it has no end"
knowing I lied.

Effortless juggler of the airy sphere of evasion,
the solid round of knowledge,
months later you came home from kindergarten,
young rabbi, to instruct me,
"It's a good thing God makes us die
or the world would be too full of us—
it's a good thing, but it's not happy."

TRYING TO TALK ABOUT SEX-II

Tonight all of the women, all of the men
who came alone to this valley
are so lonely, so hungry, so longing
we hum like appliances,
we yearn like the shy accidents of nuns,
we lean toward each other like bachelors on Thanksgiving.
None of us are thinking of sex.
I write, "I feel great resistance
to the visionary, the ecstatic, even the lyric."
The dryer in the kitchen is just warming up.
Everywhere I look in this valley, there are limits.
Running in thin air, I learn
need again, the lung's absolute hunger,
the irrelevance of will.
Do I want to be out of my mind or my body?
I want to be in another story,
a house where machines not yet invented
replace the tentative weather of eggs,
a valley cradled by mountains
that open like the curtain at eight
on desire's surprising horizon.
I'm forgetting my subject—
a form of unfaithfulness.
Instead I climb up from the valley
from the climate of touch and go,
the glistening, thick-stemmed glasses,
the tender brush of what's possible,
into these black hills, into this solitude
where nothing ravishes me but what I invent.

LAST POEM FROM SQUAW VALLEY

I am coming home to you from a wilder country,
a landscape older than the seasons of absolution,
an air I craved. Here I dared
to abandon the roads, scale rock, risk
my footing to the uncertain dust
of the crushed pine shifting beneath my steps.
Here were primrose and columbine,
violets, bruising red poppies, and rarer flowers.
Here what is most beautiful could not be named.
Here I was anointed by a certain tree's
Edenic scent. Here the air was so dry
no perfume could last, resonate from a pulse.
Here at nightfall as I climbed the hillside
the pines went rising, rising
until at the crest I reached only roots.
Here night fell, sudden and hard as rain,
and the morning light surrounded me,
an army on every rise.
Here the man I sought, enemy, lover,
shadow and brother, could not be saved.
Here I leave him, abandoned echo, fading scar,
to the canyons his ancestors rode.

PART THREE

THE METAPHYSICS OF MORNING

THE METAPHYSICS OF MORNING

Always, the hour before daybreak
the world is natural, its only sounds
the body voices of insects, then, orderly
and prescient, the beginnings of birds.
Because it is dawn, what is human
is incipient, dewy, unfolding from sleep
with the shy groans of branches, the wordless
music of petals. Nothing feline as language
rubs against legs, stretches, sharpens its claws.
Because it is morning, the day's surface
is whole, like the skin on a pan of warm milk,
thickening, not yet broken by bubbles.
We are all children; all of us could grow up
to become astronauts, jugglers, the emperors
of afternoon. All marriages are possible
as weather. Sunrise could run away
with the reckless stranger of noon.
Because it is morning, night is a place
we have left behind, and evening
what we cannot imagine.

$\mathscr{W}$AKING

Begin with a man, walking.
It is not yet dawn
but slipping out of his house
into the dark lake of streets
that pull him like a current
he discovers darkness
is not total; the sky
is a glass clouded with
approaching light.
The air is so thick
he swallows each breath.
The grasses, if he lay down in them,
would drench him.
This is the landscape
of the small and human.
The trees are deciduous, they resemble us.
The beech limbs swell in their luminous skin;
the summer's second crop
of squirrels scatter before him in the leaves.
This is the morning acorns
plummet from the high oaks,
bullets, tiny and bitter.
The houses the man walks past
are lit by the transparency
of common light.
They are caves, shells, thin walls
a creature throws up for shelter;
not the houses of architecture

forming a world that shapes us
but the small shapes we model
absently, a lump of clay
in careless fingers.
These houses are thin, they are
young women, they are the mothers
bending over babies, the fathers
stretching bodies that won't wake.
The day is seeping
into sleepers' dreams,
its small demands shrill as a child's cry.
Its urgencies
are superimposed,
images reflected on a stream
and the dream diver surfaces
from the deep world he owned,
underground mountains like breasts,
the tunnel that leads backward
to birth, forward to death,
the stone face of all our choices,
the amazing flora of wish.
Now the first blackbird barks
out of the fluttering leaves,
wakes a wave of echoing crows.
Cars flow like current,
the insect buzz swells.
A child groans and mutters, pummels
his bed, talking back
to the rulers of both worlds.
The man walking
is no longer alone.
Lighted windows solidify

the transparent walls of houses.
The world becomes a place.
At exactly the moment
when the condensing glare of the milky sky
matches the flare of the street lamps,
they cut off as if daylight were a switch.
The man walking returns
to the house he left
in another season, night;
he is panting, his body is shining
with the fine dew
it made out of morning.

Small Composition in the Colors of the Sky

"Orange," my son says, speaking
in his sleep, emphatically,
as if orange were an enemy,
a necessity.
It's such a black morning.
If there's rain it's drizzle
sifting down without sound,
a fall of darkness.
My child has slipped back
into the wash of dreams,
the vat of the world's colors.
When he wakes, will he remember
what orange means?
Over and over again
these mornings I watch
the light come into the sky
imperceptibly but
without fail: the way
all change moves around and
in us, enemy,
necessity.
I lie in my bed
slipping in and out
of something not quite
sleep, not quite waking
holding the night
my sleeping child
daylight at the window
my waking child.

$\mathcal{S}$KY

From the train, a web of light, broad slashes—
those strokes, the outrageous rhyme of white
diagonals, angry mutterings from the dark interstices
of that meeting: statement, announcement. The train
sways, halting, thick with commuters. Evening
converts their sentence from one imprisonment
to another. Morning will reverse the decision.
In each cell, there is the heavy weight of love
on the shoulders, attention to a child's cries, the pleas
of the possible, the straining engine of consciousness,
struggling to learn what's needed. Nothing is given.
In these latitudes, the day's revival is mined
from an unforgiving landscape: each night, sunrise
must be earned before day breaks. Only the sky
lifts at moments, spreads balm on daylight's wounds:
the dense perfume of a woman beautiful for years.

NINE-PART INVENTION FOR THE
MORNINGS OF CHARLES' NINTH YEAR

I.

My child's stirring, waking—a world
stirs in me too, floods me with a wash
of life, the way years ago my milk
let down at his cry. The woman who loves
and rages at this dear familiar
infuriating other wakes in my cells, my veins.

Eight years ago at this hour,
you were out of my body, swaddled
in a white blanket, held near
my head where I could look at you
while they stitched the seam cut
to let you slip into stunning light.
In the earliest photographs
my swollen breast's larger than your head;
you glance at it with wonder,
small traveller awed by mountains.
How quickly you learned the human art
of using what surrounds us: trained me
to come, lift, feed, cleanse, rock,
sing, walk, amazing repertoire
of mountains. Later you built me
into the shelter you went foraging
from, cave, hearth, bed of straw.
At two you couldn't resist biting
the milk-white shoulder, snowy slope,

and discovered avalanche: a hand
striking your cheek. Since the first
skirmishes, our battle recapitulates
history: we are lovers, enemies;
I am your home, you are my monarch;
you use and abandon me, cavalier,
terrified, fearing my death
almost as much as your own.

Right now, invading my bed, my lap,
clicking your teeth, scratching, absent, restless,
you are a soldier, willing to lay down your limbs
but not your weapons, bringing the war
into this land you scout for ambush,
hidden fortresses. As day breaks,
we are together in the trenches.

II.

A room away, I can hear you breathe,
the sound I listened longest for...
the key that released me from the gentle
bondage of my body made cradle
for the arduous journey you never make
easy or easily: from waking to sleep.
Even now you need the radio's murmur—
the ball game, music—in the dark
silence you resist dissolving into
sleep: letting yourself down into
blackness as your body settles, floats away.

Born near the equinox, you thrive on
extremes: high summer, solid winter.

Spring and fall, you breathe the mild air
and choke on pollen, leaf-mold, spreading
messengers of the news you don't want
to hear: transience, change.

III.

Five months pregnant and starting
to bleed a little. No one's sure
what it means. I dream solution:
my womb's a magic sack you can slide
out of—doctors examine you, slip
you back into your sheath. I see you:
your unborn face is like the moon's:
pale, serene, complete. You are
whole and growing. When four months later
I hold you for the first time, an hour
after the cesarean—that sesame that
opens and shuts my womb to let you
into light—your face is like the moon's.

IV.

You were the waker of this world once.
No day dawned without your crowing
it in, a laughing or crying bird of day.
Your eyes opened first, you beheld
our sleep and broke it, small sun
that woke us whatever the weather.
But nights now you are journeying
farther and farther in your dreams
and when you struggle back, swim

39

rivers, scramble over mountains,
surface from the ocean's bed,
you find us living in the morning
as if we were its originals.
You yawn, stretch. You gather yourself,
an army charged with invading day.
We are the natives who haven't a chance,
overwhelmed by awe and firepower,
by breakfast we are your subjects,
you and your weapons so clearly superior,
charmed, divinely inflicted upon us
by the benign deities of day.

V.

My son's woken up and gone back to sleep.
Small miracle—for years now, he's
not done this: waking, however early,
was absolute, allowing no return
to the kingdom of sleep until another
night fell. He is growing human,
a creature whose rhythms nature
doesn't dictate, for whom what's natural
must be discovered.

        Or am I wrong,
is he awake still, the child
to whom day is irresistible,
in whom the wish for oblivion
is still buried, undiscovered?
Awake, yawning and stretching in the dark,

playing possum, listening to the cars
swooshing over rain-slicked streets,
waiting till he can't wait any more.

I wake earlier and earlier, on the other
curve of the cycle from early waking to
later and then swinging back until
end echoes beginning: the baby, the old
woman for whom sleep and waking are
separated only by a veil of water,
dipped into over and over throughout
night, day.

       Awake or asleep
my son is growing into the hard years
of distinction, separation: night
from day, sleep from waking, dream
from act. When he slips into my bed,
dreams in my lap, I don't send him away.

VI.

You glimmer a moment
in the mirrored dark
on the door
of my lit room,
blue ghost,
little sleepwalker
flickering in the dim hall
like the blue dawn
glistening on snow.

I pretend I don't see you,
let you slip back,
burrowing animal,
to the cave of bed.

VII.

Small dreamer, now that you need me less
why am I here? You would like to skate
out onto a pond of silence alone to
the horizon and break the perfect circle,
writing your name with a shining blade.
But there I am, squatting in the hut
someone built near the bank.
I have lit a fire, heated coffee,
used my hands in the small rituals
that claim the day. You skate out
on the pond ignoring me.

VIII. INTERLUDE WITH ANGELS

Angels come climbing
into the bed where you are drinking
the aromatic first cup of morning
and opening your pen to the
unwritten pure page of the day
and they say, "Mom can you see
the knot in this piece of thread?
Mom I'm going to get back
my Roger Clemens card today,
Mom can you find the knot with your fingers?"

Angels are small, their skin
belongs to them, downy with the infinite
fine hairs of angel fur. They are never
still, they pulse and flutter,
vibrate and twitch until the bed
is incandescent with their motion.
Your coffee spills over the lip
of its cup with a lukewarm sigh.
The caress of angels is bruising;
under the angel fur they are all
small sharp bones, angelically
drawn to your belly, your breasts.
Tomorrow you will wear the mark
of angels: yellowy, sea-green,
iridescent. Angels lay their
heavy heads against your chest;
you feel the thin fast beating
of their hearts; they are whistling
Eine kleine Nachtmusik
which one of their number
composed for angels.

IX.

You are eight and a half years old
and nearly flying. In March,
the equinox of your half-birthday
finds you solemn and impish, clinging and cold,
passionate in both. You seldom curl up
in my bed first thing in the morning
but at breakfast eating cold fruit
and getting colder, you ask for

a lap not a sweater. You are launched
into your ninth year of exuberant life
on this planet. I trail you, the heavy
tail of a kite, bumping and scudding,
bruised, exhilarated.

Last night a dream gathering
of women—a circle mean as a noose—
told me how I neglect you,
letting you play alone each afternoon
in a stony concrete arena
as if you were learning to be a gladiator
in a world that bears witness
to the existence of lions.

Somewhere you are dancing
the gangly dance of skinny boys
in the streets of late afternoon,
limb and glitter, all angles.
You are free and lonely.
I am lying down somewhere,
on a couch, in a darkened room,
in a shallow box like your first cradle.
I am gathered into the dark
but I brought you to light
and the bones my body made out of
its blood lightly celebrate.

PART FOUR

DESIRE

CALIFORNIA DESERT SONG

This is such dry country.
It grows men with blue eyes
that flinch from light, mouths
tight as the furled cones of pine,
hands clenched like mule's ears
on the mountain rising
toward rain.

What kind of man are you
who would crawl in the dust
from Truckee to Reno to tease out
a single spring welling up
through the grit, the ground-down
soil and rock that is the harsh
bed of this valley?

You are the miner with opening hands.
You choose that path that leads down,
follow the water's clear shiver and
trickle under the stones.
You trail the edge of boulders.
When you come to the caves
blocked by layers of stone furled
like petals, you slip inside
like a man closing his eyes and
entering a woman he loves too much
to bear watching.

WHAT NOW?

The season is changing.
The morning is fog, a decoy.
The geese crying out while they line the sky
mar everything.
I am too new,
forming slowly, a drop of water,
a bud, a pearl.
Why do I want to stop?
At the end it's a matter of knowing
when to push.
Amazed, I find myself
at the peak, the opening,
the last stretch of sand reaching seawards.
How do I stop?
What if I go on forever
forgetting my body
like a glove
till I'm lying beside myself
and the long cadences of morning
release me?

ANALOGUES

I. FIGHTING YOUR LIFE

The stupid bird trapped in my kitchen,
beating against the window,
can't understand glass.
Smashing through would cost blood;
it doesn't see there's a door.
Dumbly, it batters itself,
trees in the wind a feast of flight
spread before it.

II. DESIRE

The body wakes
not with the single flower
of the mind's consciousness,
a burning wire, focused,
but a blossoming dense and rooted
as beds of impatiens
after a summer's spreading, a growing
season's slow domination
of the ground of the possible.

III. MARRIAGE

The fat bee in a drowse of afternoon sunlight
cruises the pink, the coral impatiens spread
from the lonely clumps of spring
into this sea, lazy as bathers, crowding out
andromeda, azalea, laurel, taking over
the terrain, pushing into bare spots,
growing through what already was planted and bloomed.
Effortless flowering owner,
you are becoming a weed.

RAVING

It's what we want:
spring and harvest together,
moon-ripe chrysanthemums among snowdrops,
thrusting Jack-in-the-pulpit,
the wild aster's wavering blue flame—
not the tyranny of growth:
blossoms ascending the gladiolus,
bottom petals tawny-edged
and wilting while
green buds clutch the tip.
Craving is better than having:
free from the law of here
leads to there, we have
the whole spear flowering at once,
unfurling every peach, cream,
pale yellow stamen-centered bloom.

Craving, I will never hold you
in my arms, our bodies cooling
in the sweet bath of our sweat,
your lips on my forehead murmuring,
feeling the world compose itself
again beneath my body—
a bed, a floor, the earth—
and know the oldest sadness, the gravity
when we are beside ourselves—
petals floating into wind—
that keeps our bodies bodies.

$\mathscr{S}$IXTH DAY

Brushing against
each other, our bodies
rustle, dry leaves
on the lawn. In the larder
the cut loaf's shrunk
to crust. Skimmed,
the milk runs blue
and thin. The fruit bowl's
cornucopia spills
one shrivelled apple,
a fistful of grapes.
There's not an egg in the house.
Over breakfast
raw words dwindle
in our throats
to the broken
speech of fingers.
When I touch you, my hand's
rough. I have just
enough blood in my veins.
When the paring
knife nicks me, the scratch
bleeds a red line thin as
the rivers' lines
on a map.
Sabbath waits like a storm.

EQUESTRIAN

The desire to sleep and sleep
and sleep—I woke to it
this morning. Once in the night
it woke me, only to take me
back into dream with the hard edge
of deliberation. As if
a voice said, "Here, want this,
want this."
The difference it makes
knowing I want—
as if "I" is just desire's body
and desire itself is wanting.

The desire to sleep again,
natural as the pull of moving water.
The body protests. The body
is not the point. The body is
where we are, not what.
Or is the body the point?
As if the equestrian
cartwheeling above her solid mount
knew suddenly she was horse,
not rider; that body her abandoned self;
and soul's triumphant levitation,
the acrobatics of a shadow.
Wake me, steed, she begs,
root me, anchor. Give me
the long lead, the pretty one;
the gentlest bit, but steel.

THREE ABOUT THE BODY

I.

The body says, if you weren't
here, tyrant, goad, itch,
I'd live like a king. Nothing
would keep me from my desires.
The body sounds omniscient,
positive as the steel smiles
of those who comfort the wounded,
holy and meretricious as a sage.

II.

The body's an old house
you've lived in too long,
familiar but cramped,
comfortable, shabby,
not really suited to the life
you are trying to live.
One of these days you will find
the power to move,
the place worth moving to.
All you will take
of the old furnishings
are the mirrors
that have seen so much
and said so little.

III.

Why do I castigate you,
shell, home, Siamese
twin? Everything sacred
enters through you.

$\mathcal{D}$ESIRE

The surface of the milk
is quiet, but slowly tiny
bubbles well up around the edge,
circle it, lace, a delicate ruff
dividing liquid from
the enamelled wall of the pan.
Keep the flame underneath
steady and the whole surface
will erupt, convulse, consume itself.
You don't need the color of flame
for this, the slow color
of gentians—serene, intense—
does it, given time,
which is all we are given,
like the silences
in music or a bolt of cloth
unrolled and spilling over
counters, wanting to fill
the whole room before
it is cut off.

PART FIVE

DISTANTIATION

DISTANTIATION

At supper my son says, "There,
it's happening again,"
and when we ask "what?",
he tells us, "my hand keeps going
small, far away."
I remember:
the pale face across the desk
becoming tiny, an actor's viewed
from the top balcony, the desk,
the room itself tunneling away—
wrong end of a telescope
was my name for it.
Does it happen innocently and teach us
its uses or is this the rare instance
of our need changing the real?
To an infant in its mother's arms
the moment must come when
the breast, the face, looming large
and close as necessity,
are hateful. And suddenly
they are tiny, far away.
One has soared like a zoom lens
in reverse to this height
at which the claustrophobic world
of love's suffering
breaks open.

*B*READ

This morning love set a table before you,
laid out a meal for you to break
your fast, provisioned you
for day, then left.

It's not enough:
the daily. I wanted wings,
flutes, the white annunciation
shattering my house.

Love is not visible,
only its works.
Wake early enough and it is
Sunday, the air sanctified
by the absence of design.
Smell warm bread, the ripe
musk of the vines. At the edge of vision,
love's white skirts are vanishing.

Stew

When I stir the pot this morning,
I don't like what the spoon pulls up.
Old stew, I should carry you
out to the backyard
in your thick iron pan
so heavy my wrists ache,
cover your steaming
surface, bubbling with old
savory smells, with a tight
black lid, dig a trench
with an iron shovel.
You will be buried treasure,
grave goods, the rich food
of another world.
You're no use any more
in this one. The dogs
drawn by your scent
to my garden are the
brown dogs of wandering,
neither enemy nor friend.
Where they are going and why
has nothing to do with me.
They belong to a different
world, like you, old stew,
and the flies that hover
and buzz over your carcass
will ride their backs
into carrion country.

$\mathcal{H}$OW WE GROW

At first what rises is simple:
hunger, thirst, a natural face.
Or how could we grow?
That rush of floating leaves,
suddenly stirred, mined with wind:
where are the stars?
Something rises in us, of us,
floods as though it were weather,
carries us out of the country
we'd settled and sowed.
Then your own hand holding
its brother plunges through
tunneling space;
remote now and tiny,
it solicits tenderness.
You are so far away you have it
to spare. Your act places you,
reveals you are
your own new relation,
connected not by marriage
or blood, but by the time-lapse
photographs of a history.
You stand next to yourself
in the risen wind.

RITHMETIC

The woman with the full life
lives with the woman with the empty life.
The woman who has a husband,
two children, a job that absorbs her
lives with the woman who is unmarried,
childless, unemployed.
The woman with no time for herself
with the woman who has nothing but time.
The woman needed too much
with the woman nobody needs.
At midnight each of them
sits in her kitchen
eating forgetfulness;
neither can ever sleep enough.
One of them plans to kill
herself; the other conceives
a third child.
They are each on the verge
of disappearing.
They live together like sisters;
they envy and misjudge each other.
They are both such womanly women;
they are both infuriating.
Add them, divide them;
marry, divorce.
Let one endow the other
with half a husband,

a share of a job, one baby and an egg;
the other bring as her dowry
a room's worth of solitude,
hours waiting to be filled.
Match-making fails:
they are members of different
species, they cannot mate,
they are twins, there
is only one of them,
there isn't one
of them at all.

THE DREAM

I am back in that apartment where I lived
the intense, limited suffering
of my twenties, twenty-five years ago.
The boy who was my husband is not there,
his absence neither questioned nor explained.
The rooms are furnished by everything
I've learned since leaving them.
The flowers, the paintings, the walls
display the white austerity of order
disciplined by art that sorrow slowly teaches.
Light fills the rooms, gladioli
blossom up like scales played legato,
with delicacy and force; the crimson shawl
tossed over a chair speaks with authority—
where except from my life could these rooms
have learned what they declare?
Nothing they tell helps me.

*I*N THE SMALL WORLD

*(after a visit to the model train
museum in Strasbourg, Pennsylvania)*

Walk through the black curtain and it is night.
The room that houses the world is barnlike and shabby,
bare planks underfoot, a worn handrail separates us
from the exhibition tables, defines the narrow passage
we are crowded into, a constricted ellipse
circling the model world. At first all you see
are myriad lights: here it is night when the world
is lit by lamplight, floodlights, streetlights,
car lights, spotlights, train lights. The darkness glistens
as in a child's night-lit room where every shadow's gilded.
In the light everything in this world is moving.
Skaters go round and round the pond; skiers ride the lift
up and their skis down over and over on the one
snowy slope. The steamboat in the amusement park
paddles back and forth its one swath of water;
the locomotive on its scaled-down track shuttles
from Strasbourg to Paradise and back, its smoke
clouding the fields where hounds chase the fox
they never catch. Tobacco fields are hoed and hoed
again; one boy flies a kite behind the barn while scouts
camping in the next wood work on their next badge,
chopping logs, shooting arrows, boxing: the badge
they will never finish. In the playground the seesaw
rocks to the drums of the approaching parade.
As the soldiers near, the children's play changes rhythm,
and what was singing goes marching. The house on fire
is conveniently next door to the firehouse. When the alarm
sounds, engines rush to it the way the ambulance

does to the accident down the block; men carry the victim
bloodily away, put out the flames; each returning
silence is broken by the scream of sirens. The circus
is in the midst of a performance: its parade
circles the streets, acrobats riding elephants;
in the big tent the high wire act is already in the air,
trapeze artists dancing toward and away from each other,
while below them seals balance tiny globes, never stopping.
Everything starts up and finishes and starts again.
No wonder there is a wedding and a funeral both.
The wedding party gathers in front of the church while
on the other side of the graveyard, a marquee,
festive and bridal, shelters the fresh bed waiting
for the flag-draped coffin, and soldiers in blue fire
seven guns into the stunning silence of old gravestones.
It is right that the only funeral is that of a soldier
whose death belongs to him the way play belongs to children
or answering alarms to firefighters or soaring from thin
wires into thin air to trapeze artists. The same soldier
is buried over and over. No one in this world is lying
in a field gazing at the sky until time stops spinning;
no one is painting a picture or carving stone;
no one steps outside the music of the many parades
to the space where music comes from to create it; no one
wrestles alone with the sense of a world moving and still
beyond him. Nothing here moves to the inexorable rhythm
which musters us to a destination outside this world
we surround and encompass like sentinels, larger than life,
with its valleys, its mountains, its long days
and short nights illuminated for beauty.
This is how we live most of the time, small
and beautifully moving as these replicas,
blind to anything but the dazzling display.

ART SIX

THE COUNTRY OF WOMEN

THE COUNTRY OF WOMEN

I. A MAN HANDS ME A ROSE

Crossing my path early one morning
a man I have never seen before
hands me a rose.
I understand:
the freshness of morning, the dew,
that bush that blossomed early
and kept blossoming all summer,
the way unbruised flowers
drifted to the lawn
in last night's fine rain
and lie there now
glistening.

A man hands me a rose,
as if to say, you are a rose.
I understand this too:
even here, in the drift of morning,
holding these petals
in my loosening hand,
my body is a rose to me.
Flower, fruit swelling,
sacred cave inviting worship;
home, field, garden, grave.
In a landscape of metaphor,
a rose apprehends itself.

II. INCEPTION

A woman leaves her house
at six in the morning,
walks into the darkness
before dawn.
In the motions of her walk,
she owns the morning.
Still she is not alone;
accompanied by the imagined
eyes of strangers,
she cannot walk down a street
except as a body
saying, "Someone can enter me,
possess me."
The pure anonymity
of a man
walking through first dawn
could exist for a woman
only in a new Eden.

III. THE COLONIZED

In my dream, a boy of fifteen writes,
"Making love to women is making
love to the colonized."

Othello speaks to Desdemona's body:
"You are the sacred cave
that comes to exist at my touch,
that did not exist before my touch,
that will cease to exist

when I cease to touch you.
If I do not own you,
you are wilderness, chaos:
your eyes the lake
I lose my face in; your breasts
the spring where drinking
I am infant again;
the dark grove of your sex
a wood where I could be
lost forever.
Mine, you sanctify my life:
you receive me, you give me
back to myself forever,
you bear witness only to me."

IV. MY REAL BODY

Just out of the shower I catch my image
in the foggy mirror:
a woman with a thick midriff,
large loose breasts, nipples relaxed
and spreading, sarong of a towel
knotted around my waist.
I'm a *National Geographic* nude:
a shock at first but so explicit
as to be utterly ordinary,
at the other pole from *Playboy*
compositions of taut curves,
erotic and ominous as desire's bow.
If this towel could flower,
would I be beautiful?
Nothing is more exotic than the real.

I have grown up and older neither
as I'd dreamed nor feared.

v. WHY A WOMAN CAN'T BE POPE

Everyone knows that under her robes,
there would be breasts,
the nipples brown raspberries,
a sloping mound, furred,
the cleft in the fur where
a tongue fits, furled layers,
lips, between them the tunnel
into the last world.

vi. THEOLOGY

The immortality of the soul and war
are twins born of one father,
male conceptions
springing as Athena did
from the head of a god.
Capital inventions:
the art of death and its sweet
poisonous antidote—the dream
of transcendence of that body,
nature, which is always a woman.

In the country of women
there is no season when birth
is not sacred. Every day celebrates
the extraordinary advent of the child

and every day accepts the crucifixion
of the child's perfection
on the cross of the human
and every day resonates
with the knowledge that
that which is rent and broken
rises again in the physical world.

VII. BIOGRAPHY

What does it mean to live
your life as a woman
in a body which opens
like a wound, bleeds
like a cut, breeds,
vulnerable and astonishing?

I have carried my sex with me
for fifty years; since I was ten,
it has defined me.
There is no such thing
as an anonymous woman.
Our bodies give us away,
mice making small sounds
in the wainscoting.

What if my back aches
or a spell spreads over me,
chill or flush, a moonwave
of intenser feeling?
They have tied my hands,
they have eaten my bread,

they have listened to nothing.
Small buds push up
like buttons on a bursting shirt.
Nothing contains this force.

VIII. THE GARDEN

A woman's husband meets her at the airport
after spring vacation and tells her
a dozen roses have come for her.
All the way home she wonders
who sent her roses; she sees them
lying in tissue paper in a long white box,
their stems stripped of thorns,
each leaf glistening, deckle-edged,
tinged with the crimson sheen
of the tight and perfect blossoms.
At home, she finds thick cardboard
cartons, in each a burlap-wrapped clump
of roots, dirt, thorny stumps
she'd ordered and forgotten
a season ago. They wait
for her digging, lugging water,
manure, lime; wait for her hands,
knees, back, her fertilizing labor.
Years from now to a man passing
the garden she's grown of them,
each thriving rose will seem
self-created, self-delighting,
effortless
as a woman's beauty.

PART SEVEN

SEASONS

Seasons

I.

I hear the small singer
of daybreak
push up notes tentative
as crocus, first snow,
hear the first crow
banish the night's breath.
The sky swells with light,
a breast filling with milk.
The long body of day
stretches and sighs.
How many ways to say
morning has come?
How many mornings
to say it?

II.

I wake and take my soundings for the day,
survey my body, ridges of old formation,
a fresh bruise on my knee, knotted muscles
in the ribs, back. In the landscape of the body
recalcitrance, an unwillingness to be used,
to bend under the day. Outside: gray drizzle,
not cold, not warm—the indifferent weather
of a world which neither loves nor hates us,

but persists, insists on existing in a limbo
we can't inform. This is the weather
we sleep against, turning from it to our indoor lives
like opening a book, getting lost in a story.

Waking and turning and waking again,
wanting not to sleep, wanting not to wake,
wanting to wake to a state more sleeping
than waking, wanting to sleep in a state
more waking than sleeping: this is the easy part.
The hard part is the story: where you were
when you got the news, what time it was,
how long it took to reach the hospital.

Today even the easiest task is too much:
to ask a favor, phone about the car,
make plans for the children, resist
telling the truth to people
who care to hear it as little as you.
Sleeping, the day weighed like the old coat
I'd thrown across the bed at the threat
of record lows. A day like this
can't be thrown off, taken lightly.
A day like this is thick with petty terrors
that dissolve by nightfall, leaving
ashes on the tongue.

III.

The heavy weather of stalled summer,
stale and exhausted, hangs on for weeks,
settled in, stolid, lasting past
its uses, refusing to loose
its grip. Autumn's wet and mild
and the leaves pile where they fall,
soaked layers, decaying,
no hard frost to shatter them,
kill the life feeding on death.

When I came into the world,
it was August.
Wintering in the womb,
cold hadn't touched me:
what did I think
when that first autumn
gathered itself at dawn
around my crib
announcing the ominous:
change.

IV.

My child can't breathe: leaf-mold,
that lovely word, necrophilus,
lover of death. An allergy chokes him:
his lungs are bellows working underwater;

87

at his chest, my ear discovers
a deep-sea world of slosh and whooze.
I'm choking too but it's not
the mold. Yesterday a friend
described her mother's collapse:
arteries blocked, the stream of
consciousness almost bursting.
I panic. I feel myself turning
colors like the leaves in their brilliant
perception of fall's imminence, feel
the tightening of that grip
which will grow brittle and snap.
I flurry into sound
like a flock of starlings
disturbed by evening.

V.

Late autumn, temperature in the upper
forties, border country between realms:
heat and cold, summer, winter, youth, age.
The light at mid-morning has ceased to amaze
itself. Spread thin, it meets
necessity like an old companion, it gives
what it cannot withhold. Trees are leafless,
only the oak clings to the subterfuge
of another season. I used to think we were
natural: grew, blossomed, became ourselves
the way acorn becomes oak. There is no pattern,
only what we make, force: the shabby and necessary
assertions of self, makeshift, original or derived,
distorted or allowing some unforeseen flowering,
never ordained, always possible.

VI.

Something opens, the way the sky did last night
after a day when wet wind flapped and arched
through the landscape, and clouds were a lid
on the wind's turmoil, the troubled, narrow weather.
The lid lifted and streaming from beneath it,
light, incandescent, a wash of it,
coming to rest on the river's surface
gleaming, unbroken, as if to say:
this is what water is for.

Why do the colors of autumn sing to me
this year as if they'd never flamed so darkly?
The leaves, double in color, gold turning coral,
yellow mottled with green, crimson veins etching
the yellow flesh of maples, seem hallucination
against the mute sullen-skied weather:
dawn opening gray doors, dusk falling without
sunset's exultation, afternoons of aluminum—
a vision hard to bear, hard to abandon.

VII.

Does the absence of birdsong
at this white hour spell rain,
small storms like the songs of a humming child,
absent, a room away? Are leaves
piled against the gutters, soaked, layered
with moisture? Is the branch punctuated
by drops, the beak of each bird a small
wet exclamation? Is the rain a spell
cast over the trees for a purpose the leaves

don't talk about, except in midwinter
when they are germs of themselves, furled
against the possibility of spring's failure?
The chords of autumn reassure, dense and solid
as sunlight hitting rock.

VIII.

Take me into the seasons,
into transformation,
into the music of growth.
What if I were changed
from the living
to the dying?
This is not change.
This morning what dying is
slips into me the way the hot coffee
I am sipping seeps slowly through
my body, spreading down, out,
a wave, breaking
at my center.
I remember a shore so cold
the last reach of the waves was etched
in ice on the frozen sand:
delicate marker of where ocean
gave up, accepted
transformation.

IX.

Take me into the seasons.
I need the crow's waking the sky;
I need the ice forming like lace
on the edges of pools,
the red leaves left hanging
to mark the season
on the trees that have given up
everything else and turned
their faces to another year.
I need the green-white buds
of the dogwood thrusting
pale fingertips
into the morning frost;
I need the geese gathering
their horns overhead, rehearsing
for flights they never perform.
I need the hoarfrost
on the wide fields bordering the waters
of the icy creek, the music
of creek bed, pebble and twig
beating in the watery rush.
Approaching light washes over me,
the cold baptism
of daily time. I shiver
on the edge of a pool
of dark water.

X.

Everything that grows turns and holds
itself at the threshhold of transformation:
the sleeper almost awake turns to his dream
with a lover's passion, the woman close to term
feels her body grow weightless, as if her burden
were air. The lightening before birth
and the lightening before death: old tales
speak of that clarity, that recovery of self
on the verge of immersion. Janus-
or crab-like, moving forward, then back,
regression always a sign of movement,
a partner in its dance.

I wake to a new season.
Overnight the wind rose, changed direction,
turned abruptly as a slamming door.
Something new-scented as grass gusts, pushes
into the night-thickened room.
Shivering, flinching, I pull up covers,
hunch into the old heat, the worn-out
weather. The crow is callously usual,
but a bird I've never heard before,
tentative, small-winged, whistles
into the breaking dark,
the broken weather.

$\mathscr{A}$BOUT THE AUTHOR

Photo by Walter G. Hagenbuch

Sandra Kohler's poetry has been published in *The American Poetry Review, Poetry Now, CALYX Journal, The Massachusetts Review, Calapooya Collage, West Branch,* and many other publications. She is the recipient of two Pennsylvania State Council on the Arts writing fellowships and is a lecturer on Creative Writing at Susquehanna University. She has taught at Bryn Mawr College, the Curtis Institute, and Prince of Wales College (Prince Edward Island) and holds a Ph.D. in English Literature from Bryn Mawr College. This is her first collection of poetry.

Selected Titles from Award-Winning CALYX Books

NONFICTION

Natalie on the Street by Ann Nietzke. A day-by-day account of the author's relationship with an elderly homeless woman who lived on the streets of Nietzke's central Los Angeles neighborhood. *PEN West Finalist!*
ISBN 0-934971-41-2, $14.95, paper; ISBN 0-934971-42-0, $24.95, cloth.

The Violet Shyness of Their Eyes: Notes from Nepal by Barbara J. Scot. A moving account of a western woman's transformative sojourn in Nepal as she reaches mid-life. PNBA Book Award.
ISBN 0-934971-35-8, $14.95, paper; ISBN 0-934971-36-6, $24.95, cloth.

In China with Harpo and Karl by Sibyl James. Essays revealing a feminist poet's experiences while teaching in Shanghai, China.
ISBN 0-934971-15-3, $9.95, paper; ISBN 0-934971-16-1, $17.95, cloth.

FICTION

The Adventures of Mona Pinsky by Harriet Ziskin. In this fantastical novel, a 65-year-old Jewish woman uncovers a complicated plot, faces alienation and ridicule, and ultimately is reborn on a heroine's journey.
ISBN 0-934971-43-9, $12.95, paper; ISBN 0-934971-44-7, $24.95, cloth.

Killing Color by Charlotte Watson Sherman. These compelling, mythical short stories by a gifted storyteller delicately explore the African-American experience. Washington State Governor's Award.
ISBN 0-934971-17-X, $9.95, paper; ISBN 0-934971-18-8, $19.95, cloth.

Mrs. Vargas and the Dead Naturalist by Kathleen Alcalá. Fourteen stories set in Mexico and the Southwestern U.S., written in the tradition of magical realism.
ISBN 0-934971-25-0, $9.95, paper; ISBN 0-934971-26-9, $19.95, cloth.

Ginseng and Other Tales from Manila by Marianne Villanueva. Poignant short stories set in the Philippines. Manila Critic's Circle National Literary Award Nominee.
ISBN 0-934971-19-6, $9.95, paper; ISBN 0-934971-20-X, $19.95, cloth.

POETRY

Open Heart by Judith Mickel Sornberger. An elegant collection of poetry rooted in a woman's relationships with family, ancestors, and the world.
ISBN 0-934971-31-5, $9.95, paper; ISBN 0-934971-32-3, $19.95, cloth.

Light in the Crevice Never Seen by Haunani-Kay Trask. The first book of poetry by an indigenous Hawaiian to be published in North America. It is a revelation about a Native woman's love for her land, and the inconsolable grief and rage that come from its destruction.
ISBN 0-934971-37-4, $11.95, paper; ISBN 0-934971-38-2, $21.95, cloth.

Raising the Tents by Frances Payne Adler. A personal and political volume of poetry, documenting a woman's discovery of her voice. Finalist, WESTAF Book Awards.
ISBN 0-934971-33-1, $9.95, paper; ISBN 0-934971-34-x, $19.95, cloth.

Black Candle: Poems about Women from India, Pakistan, and Bangladesh by Chitra Divakaruni. Lyrical and honest poems that chronicle significant moments in the lives of South Asian women. Gerbode Award.
ISBN 0-934971-23-4, $9.95, paper; ISBN 0-934971-24-2, $19.95 cloth.

Indian Singing in 20th Century America by Gail Tremblay. A brilliant work of hope by a Native American poet.
ISBN 0-934971-13-7, $9.95, paper; ISBN 0-934971-14-5, $19.95, cloth.

Idleness Is the Root of All Love by Christa Reinig, translated by Ilze Mueller. These poems by the prize-winning German poet accompany two older lesbians through a year together in love and struggle.
ISBN 0-934971-21-8, $10, paper; ISBN 0-934971-22-6, $18.95, cloth.

ANTHOLOGIES

The Forbidden Stitch: An Asian American Women's Anthology edited by Shirley Geok-lin Lim, et al. The first Asian American women's anthology. American Book Award.
ISBN 0-934971-04-8, $16.95, paper; ISBN 0-934971-10-2, $32, cloth.

Women and Aging, An Anthology by Women edited by Jo Alexander, et al. The only anthology that addresses ageism from a feminist perspective. A rich collection of older women's voices.
ISBN 0-934971-00-5, $15.95, paper; ISBN 0-934971-07-2, $28.95, cloth.

ORDER INFORMATION

CALYX Books are available to the trade from Consortium and other major distributors and jobbers.

Individuals may order direct from CALYX Books, P.O. Box B, Corvallis, OR 97339. Send check or money order in U.S. currency; add $2.00 postage for first book, $.75 each additional book.

CALYX, A Journal of Art and Literature by Women

CALYX, A Journal of Art and Literature by Women, has showcased the
work of over two thousand women artists and writers since 1976.
Committed to providing a forum for *all* women's voices, *CALYX*
presents diverse styles, images, issues, and themes that women writers
and artists are exploring.

*"The work you do brings dignity, intelligence, and a sense of wholeness to
the world. I am only one of many who bows respectfully—to all of you and
to your work."*
—Barry Lopez

"It is heartening to find a women's publication such as CALYX *which is
devoted to the very best art and literature of the contemporary woman. The
editors have chosen works which create images of forces that control
women; others extol the essence of every woman's existence."*
—Vicki Behem, *Literary Magazine Review*

"Thank you for all your good and beautiful work."
—Gloria Steinem

Published in June and November; three issues per volume.

Single copy rate: $8.00.
Subscription rate for individuals: $18/1 volume.

CALYX Journal is available to the trade from Ingram Periodicals and
other major distributors.

CALYX is committed to producing books of
literary, social, and feminist integrity.

CALYX Journal is available at your local bookstore or direct from:

CALYX, Inc., P.O. Box B, Corvallis, OR 97339

*CALYX, Inc., is a nonprofit organization with a 501(C)(3) status.
All donations are tax deductible.*

$\mathcal{C}$OLOPHON

The body text is set in 11 point Century Old Style.
Poem titles are set in 13 point Americana, small caps,
with 42 point initial capitals in Palace Script.
Typeset, layout, and production provided by
ImPrint Services, Corvallis, Oregon.